Courtesy of Wikipedia

Photograph of a crowd outside the New York Stock Exchange after the crash – 1929

Photograph of unemployed men waiting outside a soup kitchen in Chicago – February 1931

Courtesy of National Archives & Records Administration

FREE SOUP, COFFEE & DOUGHNUTS FOR THE UNEMPLOYED

FREE SOUP

HORAN BAILIFF

Photograph of a crowd at New York's American Union Bank during a bank run early in the Great Depression – 1931

Photograph of President Franklin D. Roosevelt talking to a farmer in Warm Springs, Georgia – 1932

Photograph of workers in the Civilian Conservation Corps constructing a road – 1933

Courtesy of the Franklin D. Roosevelt Library and Museum

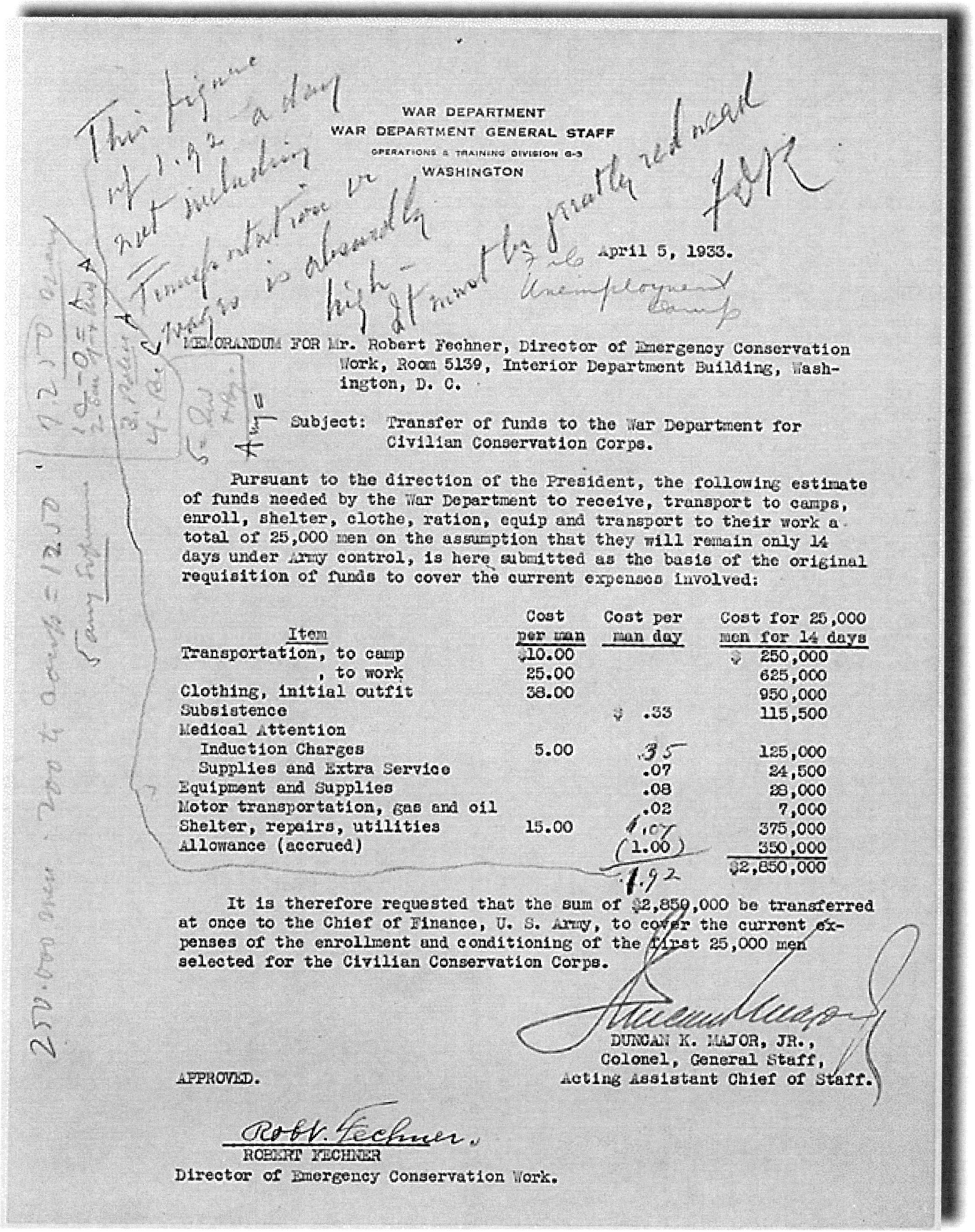

WAR DEPARTMENT
WAR DEPARTMENT GENERAL STAFF
OPERATIONS & TRAINING DIVISION G-3
WASHINGTON

April 5, 1933.

[handwritten notes in margins: "This figure of 1.92 a day not including Transportation or — wages is absurdly high — It must be greatly reduced FDR" and "Unemployment Camp"]

MEMORANDUM FOR Mr. Robert Fechner, Director of Emergency Conservation Work, Room 5139, Interior Department Building, Washington, D. C.

Subject: Transfer of funds to the War Department for Civilian Conservation Corps.

Pursuant to the direction of the President, the following estimate of funds needed by the War Department to receive, transport to camps, enroll, shelter, clothe, ration, equip and transport to their work a total of 25,000 men on the assumption that they will remain only 14 days under Army control, is here submitted as the basis of the original requisition of funds to cover the current expenses involved:

Item	Cost per man	Cost per man day	Cost for 25,000 men for 14 days
Transportation, to camp	$10.00		$ 250,000
, to work	25.00		625,000
Clothing, initial outfit	38.00		950,000
Subsistence		$ .33	115,500
Medical Attention			
Induction Charges	5.00	.35	125,000
Supplies and Extra Service		.07	24,500
Equipment and Supplies		.08	28,000
Motor transportation, gas and oil		.02	7,000
Shelter, repairs, utilities	15.00	1.07	375,000
Allowance (accrued)		(1.00)	350,000
		1.92	$2,850,000

It is therefore requested that the sum of $2,850,000 be transferred at once to the Chief of Finance, U. S. Army, to cover the current expenses of the enrollment and conditioning of the first 25,000 men selected for the Civilian Conservation Corps.

DUNCAN K. MAJOR, JR.,
Colonel, General Staff,
Acting Assistant Chief of Staff.

APPROVED.

Rob't. Fechner

ROBERT FECHNER
Director of Emergency Conservation Work.

Letter regarding the funding for the Civilian Conservation Corps – April 5, 1933

Photograph of President Franklin D. Roosevelt signing the Social Security Act of 1935 – August 14, 1935

Photograph of a "Hoover wagon" – used by farmers to save on gasoline – 1935

Photograph of Oklahoma Dust Bowl refugees – San Fernando, California – June 1935

More Oklahomans reach Calif. via the cotton fields of Ariz.

Courtesy of Library of Congress

Photograph of Florence Thompson with several of her children during the Dust Bowl – entitled "Migrant Mother" – February 1936

Courtesy of Library of Congress

Photograph of a farmer and his sons walking in a dust storm – Cimarron County, Oklahoma – April 1936

Photograph of buried machinery in Dallas, South Dakota, during the Dust Bowl – May 13, 1936

Courtesy of United States Department of Agriculture

Courtesy of Library of Congress

Photograph of a poor mother and her children during the Great Depression – Elm Grove, California – August 1936

Photograph of construction on the Bonneville Power & Navigation Dam in Oregon –
Public Works Administration project – October 24, 1936

Courtesy of the Franklin D. Roosevelt Library and Museum

Poster advertising Social Security benefits – 1938

Photograph of William Gropper's "Construction of a Dam" mural – 1939

Courtesy of the U.S. Department of the Interior

Photograph of an anti-relief protest sign near Davenport, Iowa – 1940

THIS FARMER IS NOT ON GOVERNMENT RELIEF

Courtesy of Library of Congress

Advertisement for the Workers Service Program in Rockford, Illinois – part of the Work Projects Administration – 1941

Photograph of a girl pumping water from a well that is her town's sole water supply – project of the Tennessee Valley Authority – 1942

Courtesy of Franklin D. Roosevelt Presidential Library and Museum

THE TENNESSEE VALLEY

GILBERTSVILLE DAM

PICKWICK LANDING DAM
WILSON DAM
WHEELER DAM
GUNTERSVILLE DAM
CHICKAMAUGA DAM
NORRIS DAM
WATTS BAR DAM
FORT LOUDEN DAM
HIWASSEE DAM
FONTANA DAM

M I S S.
A L A.
G A.
T E N N.
K Y.
V A.
N. C.
S. C.

Nashville
Atlanta
Birmingham

Map of the Tennessee Valley Authority – 1942

GREAT DEPRESSION & NEW DEAL
Primary Sources

Historical Documents • Maps • Photographs • Political Cartoons

INCLUDES 20 PRIMARY SOURCE DOCUMENTS:

- Photograph of a crowd outside the New York Stock Exchange after the crash – 1929

- Photograph of unemployed men waiting outside a soup kitchen in Chicago – February 1931

- Photograph of a crowd at New York's American Union Bank during a bank run early in the Great Depression – 1931

- Photograph of President Franklin D. Roosevelt talking to a farmer in Warm Springs, Georgia – 1932

- Photograph of workers in the Civilian Conservation Corps constructing a road – 1933

- Letter regarding the funding for the Civilian Conservation Corps – April 5, 1933

- Photograph of President Franklin D. Roosevelt signing the Social Security Act of 1935 – August 14, 1935

- Photograph of a "Hoover wagon" – used by farmers to save on gasoline – 1935

- Photograph of Oklahoma Dust Bowl refugees – San Fernando, California – June 1935

- Photograph of Florence Thompson with several of her children during the Dust Bowl – entitled "Migrant Mother" – February 1936

- Photograph of a farmer and his sons walking in a dust storm – Cimarron County, Oklahoma – April 1936

- Photograph of buried machinery in Dallas, South Dakota, during the Dust Bowl – May 13, 1936

- Photograph of a poor mother and her children during the Great Depression – Elm Grove, California – August 1936

- Photograph of construction on the Bonneville Power & Navigation Dam in Oregon – Public Works Administration project – October 24, 1936

- Poster advertising Social Security benefits – 1938

- Photograph of William Gropper's "Construction of a Dam" mural – 1939

- Photograph of an anti-relief protest sign near Davenport, Iowa – 1940

- Advertisement for the Workers Service Program in Rockford, Illinois – part of the Work Projects Administration – 1941

- Photograph of a girl pumping water from a well that is her town's sole water supply – project of the Tennessee Valley Authority – 1942

- Map of the Tennessee Valley Authority – 1942

Build Higher-Order Thinking Skills:

- Analysis
- Critical Thinking
- Point of View
- Compare and Contrast
- Order of Events
- & Much More!

Perfect for Gallery Walks & Literature Circles!

Great for Research & Reference!

GALLOPADE

ISBN-13: 978-0-635-10843-2

90000

9 780635 108432

7 10430 10704 9